LANGUAGE IS A MIGHTY LORD:

A Gorgias Reader

Edited by Andrew J. Patrick

ISBN: 0615658806
ISBN-13: 978-0615658803

DEDICATION

To all sophists, whether intentional or not

.

INTRODUCTION:

WHY GORGIAS MATTERS

By the standards of our age, Gorgias does not matter. He lived a long time ago, in a civilization that we nod to as the forerunner of our own, but know little about. His surviving writings are few and fragmentary. The major thinkers of his day – by which we mean Plato and Aristotle – thought him an amusing but dangerous fool. Only classicists and the occasional grad student required to take a course on rhetoric will ever hear of him.

I created this book because I am one such student. I read Gorgias as part of a graduate seminar on Rhetoric as part of the pursuit of a Master's Degree in Writing. I found *The Encomium of Helen* so amusing that I did my research paper/rhetorical analysis on Gorgias. I was sufficiently inspired to write it as a parody/tribute/apologia for the old fraud, entitled "An Encomium of Gorgias." You will find it at the end of this volume, where it doubtless belongs.

This book does not pretend to be the last or even a complete work of scholarship on the works or significance of Gorgias of Leontini. Any classicist can discourse upon the facts of his life and the significance of his work better than I can. Rather, I created this book because I decided that Gorgias, and his witty meditations upon language and truth, deserve a volume of their own. It is a tribute to the durability of the sophists, and a consideration of the value of rhetoric.

We do not like rhetoric. We do not like its practitioners. We suspect them of making the worse appear the better argument. We make jokes about 500 of them dead at the bottom of the ocean being a good start. But we cannot rid ourselves of this deeply suspicious art, and we do not know why.

Aristotle offers an explanation, near the beginning of the *Rhetoric*:

> *Rhetoric is useful because things that are true and things that are just have a natural tendency to prevail over their opposites, so that if the decisions of judges are not what they ought to be, the defeat must be blamed accordingly. Moreover, before some audiences not even the possession of the exactest knowledge will make it easy for what we say to produce conviction.*[1]

---

[1] Aristotle *Rhetoric* I.1.1355ª.20

We rely upon rhetoric for those times when the truth is not obvious to all: traditionally, matters of law, public policy, and public opinion. We cannot *know* categorically whether a man on trial is innocent or guilty, hence the ambiguous standard of "beyond a reasonable doubt." We cannot *know* which public policy will bring about the best outcome; we can only make educated guesses based on *analogous* circumstances from the past. So we need rhetoric to convince our fellows that what we think is *probably* true.

Analogy and probability are not bedrock; they are lifeboats in an ocean of doubt, and sometimes they founder. So rhetoric tends to the passionate: we argue not with surety, but as the shipwrecked clinging to the only thing they have. In the heat of passion, it serves us to be reminded of how thin and small our words really are in comparison to Actual Truth, so often unsaid and unknown. Gorgias reminds us of this, wittily and intelligently:

> *All who have and do persuade people of things do so by molding a false argument. For if all men on all subjects had both memory of things past and awareness of things present and foreknowledge of the future, speech would not be similarly similar, since as things are now it is not easy for them to recall the past nor to consider the present nor to predict the future. So that on most subjects most men take opinion as counselor but since opinion is slippery and insecure it casts those employing it into slippery and enclosed successes.*[2]

That is why he matters.

Gorgias did not invent the idea of the gulf between inward truth and expressed opinion; we find it in the Pre-Socratics as far back as Xenophanes:

> *And the clear truth no man has seen nor will anyone know concerning the gods and about all the things of which I speak;*
> *for even if he should actually manage to say what is the case,*
> *nevertheless he himself does not know it; but belief is found over all.*[3]

This thought finds its echo in Gorgias' *On Nature, Or What is Not*, presented in its surviving summary form in this volume. Gorgias parodies Parmenides and his school, particularly Melissus of Samos:

---

[2] Gorgias, *An Encomium of Helen 11*
[3] Sextus Empirucs, *Against the Mathematicians* VII 49

Whatever existed always existed and always will exist. For if it came into being, then necessarily before coming into being it was nothing. Now if it was nothing it will in no way have come to be anything before being nothing.[4]

Gorgias turns this seemingly elementary logic on its head, arguing that everything that exists fails to meet Parmenides' criteria, thus, nothing exists. Cheekiness of this kind is what earned the Sophists their seditious reputation, but to cast the Sophists as in rebellion against the Pre-Socratics overstates matters. Each of the Pre-Socratics rebelled against the one before him, offering a new understanding of the root nature of the universe. To argue and overturn the old was the normal run of things. Or, as Empedocles of Acragas put it:

Double is the generation of mortal things, and double their passing away:
the one is born and destroyed by the congregation of everything,
the other is nurtured and flies apart as they grow apart again.
And these will never cease their continual change,
now coming together by Love all into one,
now again being carried apart by the hatred of Strife.[5]

What is true of mortal things can certainly be true of mortal ideas, and mortal expressions of them. Which means that the Sophists in general, and Gorgias in particular, had a role to play in the evolution of those ideas.

What one discovers in reading Gorgias' extant texts is how they revolve around a single idea, which might be called a Sophistic Philosophy of Language: that Words and Persuasion are powerful, even divinely ordained, but they are not Truth. The *Encomium of Helen* speaks to the power of persuasive language to rule a human mind; the *Palamedes* laments the ease with which falsehood can use this power; and *On Nature* demonstrates that power's ability to overthrow all our categories

---

[4] Simplicius, *Commentary on the* Physics 162.23-26
[5] Simplicius, 157.27-30

The *Helen* remains Gorgias most famous speech, in no small part to the sheer gall of it. Helen of Troy, in fleeing her husband Menelaus for Paris (whom Gorgias refers to as Alexander), not only inaugurated a fearsome and destructive war that brought about the end of an age, she violated every standard of rectitude expected of a Greek wife. For Gorgias to argue that Helen was innocent, even if motivated by pretty words or her body's lust, was a rather frightening demonstration of his statement, contained therein: "Speech is a powerful Lord."

The *Palamedes* also draws from the tale of the Trojan War, if not from the Iliad.[6] Palamedes, prince of the Nauplians, was sent by Agamemnon to hold Odysseus to his oath to fight for Menelaus' marriage. Odysseus feigned insanity, but Palamedes would not be put off. In revenge, Odysseus planted gold and a false letter from the Trojans in Palamedes' tent. Palamedes was judged a traitor and put to death by Odysseus and Diomedes. This story, well known to Greeks of that time, gives Gorgias an opportunity to again warn of the persuasive power of false speech. In the speech, Palamedes is rational, forceful, and exhortative:

> *That you have no knowledge of your accusations is clear. Hence they must be conjectural, and you are the most villainous of men, to bring a capital charge relying on opinion—which is a most unreliable thing—and not knowing the truth. Conjecture is open to all in everything, and you are no wiser than anyone else in this. One must believe, not conjecture, but truth.*[7]

This eloquence, with truth on its side, avails him nothing: the audience knows that the Greeks will not believe him. Lie defeats truth.

However, Gorgias does not deny the possibility of truth, nor does he argue that truth is subjectively *created* by language. In this, at least, he departs from the Post-Moderns.[8] Rather, he writes, persuasively, on the difference between what is and what can be spoken. The *Palamedes* devotes a good deal of its force to this difference. Palamedes, despite his fate, knows what is true.

---

[6] Ovid mentions Palamedes in the *Metamorphoses*, as does Virgil in the *Aeneid* and Plato in the *Apology*. Homer, however does not.

[7] Gorgias, *The Defense of Palamedes* 8

[8] Such as Stanley Fish, who considers himself a "contemporary Sophist."

So Gorgias' point is not that speech may be used to make and reinforce whatever truth seems good to you. Rather, he declares that speech may be true or it may be false, but it *is*, and possesses a power over what men can do. Speech thus becomes a weapon, which, whether we like it or not, we are better off knowing how to use.

This is essentially Aristotle's assessment of rhetoric, and if we are honest, ours.

The remaining selection, the *Epitaphios*, is a funeral oration over the bodies of Athenian dead that may or may not have been a parody, and may or may not have inspired Plato to write his own epitaph parody, the *Menexenus*. I leave the question to the readers.

-Andrew J. Patrick
August 12, 2012

Language is a Mighty Lord

Andrew J. Patrick

AN ENCOMIUM OF HELEN

1. What is becoming to a city is manpower, to a body beauty, to a soul wisdom, to an action virtue, to a speech truth, and the opposites of these are unbecoming. Man and woman and speech and deed and city and object should be honored with praise if praiseworthy and incur blame if unworthy, for it is an equal error and mistake to blame the praisable and to praise the blamable. **2.** It is the duty of one and the same man both to speak the needful rightly and to refute {the unrightfully spoken. This it is right to refute} those who rebuke Helen, a woman about whom the testimony of inspired poets has become univocal and unanimous as had the ill omen of her name, which has become a reminder of misfortunes. For my part, by introducing some reasoning into my speech, I wish to free the accused of blame and, having reproved her detractors as prevaricators and proved the truth, to free her from their ignorance.

3. Now it is not unclear, not even to a few, that in nature and in blood the woman who is the subject of this speech is preeminent among preeminent men and women. For it is clear that her mother was Leda, and her father was in fact a god, Zeus, but allegedly a mortal, Tyndareus, of whom the former was shown to be her father because he was and the latter was disproved because he was said to be, and the one was the most powerful of men and the other the lord of all.

4. Born from such stock, she had godlike beauty, which taking and not mistaking, she kept. In many did she work much desire for her love, and her one body was the cause of bringing together many bodies for men thinking great thoughts for great goals, of whom some had greatness of wealth, some the glory of ancient nobility, some the vigor of personal agility, some command of acquired knowledge. And all came because of a passion which loved to conquer and a love of honor which was unconquered. **5.** Who it was and why and how he sailed away, taking Helen as his love, I shall not say. To tell the knowing what they know shows it is right but brings no delight. Having now gone beyond the time once set for my speech, I shall go on to the beginning of my future speech, and I shall set forth the causes through which it was likely that Helen's voyage to Troy should take place.

6. For either by will of Fate and decision of the gods and vote of Necessity did she do what she did, or by force reduced or by words seduced {or by love possessed}. Now if through the first, it is right for the responsible one to be held responsible; for god's predetermination cannot be hindered by human premeditation. For it is the nature of things, not for the strong to be hindered by the weak, but for the weaker to be ruled and drawn by the stronger, and for the stronger to lead and the weaker to follow. God is a stronger force than man in might and in wit and in other ways. If then one must place blame on Fate, and on a god, one must free Helen from disgrace.

7. But if she was raped by violence and illegally assaulted and unjustly insulted, it is clear that the raper, as the insulter, did the wronging, and the raped, as the insulted, did the suffering. It is right then for the barbarian who undertook a barbaric undertaking in word and in law and deed to meet with blame in word, exclusion in law, and punishment in deed. And surely it is proper for a woman raped and robbed of her country and deprived of friends to be pitied rather than pilloried. He did the great deeds; she suffered them. It is just therefore to pity her but to hate him.

8. But if it was speech which persuaded her and deceived her heart, not even to this is it difficult to make an answer and to banish blame as follows. Speech is a powerful lord, which by means of the finest and most invisible body effects the divinest works: it can stop fear and banish grief and create joy and nurture pity. I shall show how this is the case, since **9.** it is necessary to offer proof to the opinion of my hearers: I both deem and define all poetry as speech with meter. Fearful shuddering and tearful pity and grievous longing come upon its hearers, and at the actions and physical sufferings of others in good fortunes and in evil fortunes, through the agency of words, the soul is wont to experience a suffering of its own. But come, I shall turn from one argument to another. **10.** Sacred incantations sung with words are bearers of pleasure and banishers of pain, for, merging with opinion in the soul, the power of the incantation is wont to beguile it and persuade it and alter it by witchcraft. There have been discovered two arts of witchcraft and magic: one consists of errors of the soul and the other of deceptions of opinion. **11.** All who have and do persuade people of things do so by molding a false argument. For if all men on all subjects had {both} memory of things past and {awareness} of things present and foreknowledge of the future, speech would not be similarly similar, since as things are now it is not easy for them to recall the past nor to consider the present nor to predict the future. So that on most subjects most men take opinion as counselor to their soul, but since opinion is slippery and insecure it casts those employing it into slippery and insecure successes. **12.** What cause then prevents the conclusion that Helen similarly, against her will, might have come under the influence of speech, just as if ravished by the force of the mighty? For it was possible to see how the force of persuasion prevails; persuasion has the form of necessity, but it does not have the same power. For speech constrained the soul, persuading it which it persuaded, both to believe the things said and to approve the things done. The persuader, like a constrainer, does the wrong and the persuaded, like the constrained, in speech is wrongly charged.

13. To understand that persuasion, when added to speech, is wont also to impress the soul as it wishes, one must study: first, the words of astronomers who, substituting opinion for opinion, taking away one but creating another, make what is incredible and unclear seem true to the eyes of opinion; then, second, logically necessary debates in which a single speech, written with art, but not spoken with truth, bends a great crowd and persuades; {and} third, the verbal disputes of philosophers, in which the swiftness of thought is also shown making the belief in an opinion subject to easy change. **14.** The effect of speech upon the condition of the soul is comparable to the power of drugs over the nature of bodies. For just as different drugs dispel different secretions from the body, and some bring an end to disease and others to life, so also in the case of speeches, some distress, other delight, some cause fear, others make the hearers bold, and some drug and bewitch the soul with a kind of evil persuasion.

15. It has been explained that if she was persuaded by speech she did not do wrong but was unfortunate. I shall discuss the fourth cause in a fourth passage. For if it was love which did all these things, there will be no difficulty in escaping the charge of the sin which is alleged to have taken place. For the things we see do not have the nature which we wish them to have, but the nature which each actually has. through sight the soul receives an impression even in its inner features. **16.** When belligerents in war buckle on their warlike accouterments of bronze and steel, some designed for defense, others for offense, if the sight sees this, immediately it is alarmed and it alarms the soul, so that often men flee, panic-stricken, from future danger {as though it were} present. For strong as is the habit of obedience to the law, it is ejected by fear resulting from sight, which coming to a man causes him to be indifferent both to what is judged honorable because of the law and to the advantage to be derived from victory. **17.** It has happened that people, after having seen frightening sights, have also lost presence of mind for the present moment; in this way fear extinguishes and excludes thought. and many have fallen victim to useless labor and dread diseases and hardly curable madnesses. In this way the sight engraves upon the mind images of things which have been seen. And many frightening impressions linger, and what lingers is exactly analogous to {what is} spoken. **18.** Moreover, whenever pictures perfectly create a single figure and form from many colors and figures, they delight the sight, while the creation of statues and the production of works of art furnish a pleasant sight to the eyes. Thus it is natural for the sight to grieve for some things and to long for others, and much love and desire for many objects and figures is engraved in many men. **19.** If, therefore, the eye of Helen, pleased by the figure of Alexander, present to her soul eager desire and contest of love, what wonder? If, {being} a god, {love has} the divine power of the gods, how could a lesser being refuse it? But if it is a desease of human origin and a fault of the soul, it should not be blamed as a sin, but regarded as an affliction. For she came, as she did come, caught in the net of Fate, not bey the plans of the mind, and by the constraints of love, not by the devices of art.

20. How then can one regard blame of Helen as just, since she is utterly acquitted of all charge, whether she did what she did through falling in love or persuaded by speech or ravished by force or constrained by divine constraint?

21. I have by means of speech removed disgrace from a woman; I have observed the procedure which I set up at the beginning of the speech; I have tried to end the injustice of blame and the ignorance of opinion; I wished to write a speech which would be a praise of Helen and a diversion to myself.

Andrew J. Patrick

THE DEFENSE OF PALAMEDES

1. *To the Jury:* This trial is concerned not with death, which comes to all, but with honor: whether I am to die justly or unjustly, under a load of disgrace.

You have the power to decide the issue; you can kill me easily if you wish, whereas I am powerless.

If the accuser Odysseus were bringing the charge because he knew or believed me to be betraying Greece to the barbarians, he would be the best of men, as ensuring the safety of his country, his parents and all Greece, as well as the punishment of the traitor. But if he has concocted this charge through malice, he is equally the worst of men.

2. Where shall I begin my defense? A cause unsupported by proof engenders fear, and fear makes speech difficult, unless truth and necessity instruct me—teachers more productive of risk than of the means of help.

The accuser cannot know for certain that I committed the crime, because I know for certain that I did not. But if he is acting on conjecture, I can prove in two ways that he is wrong.

3. First, I cannot have committed the crime. Treasonable action must begin with discussion; but discussion implies a meeting, which was impossible since no one could come to me and I could not go to anyone, nor could a written message be sent.

Nor was direct communication possible between myself, a Greek, and the enemy, a barbarian, since we did not understand each other's language, and an interpreter would have meant having an accomplice.

4. But even supposing communication could have been arranged, it would have been necessary to exchange pledge, such as hostages (which was impossible), or perhaps money. A small sum would not have sufficed in such a great undertaking; a large sum could not have been transported without the help of many confederates.

Conveyance of money would have been impossible at night because of the guards, and by daylight because all could see. Nor could I have gone out, or the enemy have come into the camp.

Nor could I have concealed any money received.

5. But suppose all this achieved—communication established and pledges exchanged—action had then to follow. This had to be done with or without confederates. If with confederates, were they free or slaves? If any free man has information, let him speak. Slaves are always untrustworthy: They accuse voluntarily to win freedom, and also under compulsion when tortured.

Nor could the enemy have entered by my help, either by the gates or over the walls, because of the guards; nor could I have breached the walls, as in camp everybody sees everything. Therefore all such action was completely impossible for me.

6. What motive could I have had? Absolute power over ourselves or the barbarians? The former is impossible in view of your courage, wealth, prowess of body and mind, control of cities.

Rulership over the barbarian is equally impossible. I could not have seized it or won it by persuasion, nor would they have handed it to me voluntarily: no one would choose slavery instead of kingship, the worst instead of the best.

Nor was wealth my motive. I have moderate means, and do not need more. Wealth is needed by those who spend much; not by those who are masters of their natural pleasures, but by those who are enslaved by pleasures, or wish to buy honor with riches. I call you to witness that my past life proves me not to be one of these.

My motive cannot have been ambition: honor accrues to virtue, not to a betrayer of Greece. Besides, I had honor already, from you for my wisdom.

Safety cannot have been the motive. The traitor is the enemy of all: law, justice, the gods, his fellow-men.

Another motive could be the desire to help friends and injure enemies; but I would have been doing the reverse.

The remaining possibility would be a wish to avoid trouble or danger. But if I betrayed Greece, I should have betrayed myself and all that I had.

My life would have been unbearable in Greece; and if I stayed among the barbarians, I would have thrown away all the rewards of my past labors, through my own action, which is worst.

The barbarians too would have distrusted me; and if one loses credit, life is intolerable. The loss of money or throne or country can be retrieved; but the loss of credit is irretrievable.

It is thus proved that I neither could nor would have, betrayed Greece.

7. *To the Accuser:* I now address my accuser: do you base your accusation on knowledge or conjecture? If on knowledge, either this is your own or hearsay. If it is your own, give exact details of time, place, method; if hearsay, produce your witness.

It is your place to produce witnesses, not mine: no witness can be produced for what did not happen; but for what did happen, it is easy and essential to produce witnesses. But you cannot produce even false witnesses.

8. That you have no knowledge of your accusations is clear. Hence they must be conjectural, and you are the most villainous of men, to bring a capital charge relying on opinion—which is a most unreliable thing—and not knowing the truth. Conjecture is open to all in everything, and you are no wiser than anyone else in this. One must believe, not conjecture, but truth.

9. You are accusing me of two opposites, wisdom and madness: wisdom in that I am crafty, clever, resourceful; madness in that I wished to betray Greece. It is madness to attempt what is impossible, disadvantageous, disgraceful injurious to friends and helpful to enemies, and likely to make one's life intolerable. But how can one believe a man who in the same speech, to the same audience, says the exact opposite about the same things?

Do you consider the wise to be foolish or sensible? If you say 'foolish', this is original but untrue. If 'sensible' then sensible men do not commit the greatest crimes, or prefer evil to the good they have. If I am wise, I did not err. If erred, I am not wise. Therefore you are proved a liar on both counts.

I could bring counter-accusations, but I will not. I would rather seek acquittal through my virtues than your vices.

10. *To the Jury:* I must now speak of myself, in a way that would not be suitable except to one accused. I submit my past life to your scrutiny. If I mention my good deeds, I pray that no one will resent this: it is necessary in order that I may refute serious charges with a true statement of merits known to you.

Above all, my past life has been blameless. My accuser can bring no proof of this charge, so that his speech is unsubstantiated obloquy.

I claim also to be a benefactor of Greece, present and future, by reason of my inventions, in tactics, law, letters (the tool of memory), measures (arbiters of business dealings), number (the guardian of property), beacon-fires (the best and swiftest messengers), and the game of draughts as a pastime.

I mention these things to show that in devoting my thoughts to them I am bound to abstain from wicked deeds.

I deserve no punishment from young or old. I have been considerate to the old, helpful to the young, without envy of the prosperous, merciful to the distressed; not despising poverty, nor preferring wealth to virtue; useful in counsel, active in war, fulfilling commands, obeying the rulers. But it is not for me to praise myself; I do so under the compulsion of self-defense.

11. Lastly I shall speak of you to you. Lamentations, prayers, and the petitions of friends are useful when judgment depends on the mob; but before you, the foremost of the Greeks, I need not use these devices, but only justice and truth.

You must not heed words rather than facts, nor prefer accusations to proof, nor regard a brief period as more instructive than a long one, nor consider calumny more trustworthy than experience. Good men avoid all wrong-doing, but above all what cannot be mended; things can be righted by forethought, but are irrevocable by afterthought. This happens when men are trying a fellow-man on a capital charge, as you now are.

If words could bring the truth of deeds clearly and certainly before their hearers, judgment would be easy; since this is not so, I ask you to preserve my life, await the passage of time, and pass your judgment with truth. You run the great risk of a reputation for injustice; to good men, death is preferable to a bad reputation: one is the end of life, the other is a disease in life.

If you put me to death unjustly, you will bear the blame in the eyes of all Greece, as I am not unknown and you are famous. The blame will be yours, not my accuser's, because the issue is in your hands. There could be no greater crime than if you as Greeks put to death a Greek, an ally, benefactor of yours and of Greece, when you can show no cause.

Here I stop. A summary of a long speech is worth while when one is speaking to a jury of inferiors; but before the leaders of Greece it is uncalled-for, as is the exhortation to pay attention or to remember what has been said.

Language is a Mighty Lord

Andrew J. Patrick

ON NATURE, OR WHAT IS NOT

I. NOTHING EXISTS

If anything exists, it must be Being, Not-Being, or both. But it cannot be any of these.

It cannot be Non-Being; Non-Being does not exist. Hence, what exists cannot be Non-Being.

It cannot be both. It cannot be Non-Being ;Hence, it cannot be both.

It cannot be Being. If it were Being, it must be everlasting (eternal), created (temporal), or both .

It is not temporal; if it is temporal, then it has a beginning. Thus it came from what is not Being (i.e., Non-Being). But Non-Being does not exist, hence, it is not temporal .

It is not both. It cannot be either eternal or temporal. Hence, it cannot be both.

It is not eternal ; if it is eternal, then it has no beginning. Therefore it is without limit (apeiras) and so boundless. Therefore it has no position.

To have a position is to be contained in something. But to be boundless is not to be so contained. A container is larger than what it holds, But nothing is larger than the boundless. Hence, the boundless is not contained. Hence, it has no position.

Therefore it is nowhere. But to exist is to be somewhere. Hence, it is not eternal .

In addition, it cannot be one. If something exists, it has size. But what has size can be divided into infinitely many things. And even if not infinite, tripartite with length, breadth, and depth. Hence, it cannot be one.

In addition, it cannot be many. The many is made up of the addition of ones, but the one does not exist. Hence, it cannot be many.

Hence, nothing exists.

II. If Anything Does Exist, It Is Incomprehensible

The human mind can conceive of Non-Beings. The human mind can conceive of a chariot running on the sea or of a winged man. Such things do not exist and are not realities; they are Non-Beings. Hence, the human mind can conceive of Non-Beings.

Therefore Non-Being is the object of human thought (just as light is the object of sight, and sound is the object of hearing). But if Non-Being is the object of human thought, then Being is not the object of human thought. Hence, the human mind is not to be trusted with Being (as the eyes are trusted with light, and the ears trusted with sound) and so existing things cannot be thought—they can only be witnessed by the senses.

III. If Anything is Comprehensible, It Is Incommunicable

What exists is perceptible and there are no interchanges between different perceptions.

For instance, that which is seen is apprehended by the perceptions of sight, that which is heard is apprehended by the perceptions of hearing. There is no way that one could see sound or hear light.

Communication is about speech (logos), not about the things that exist. That which we communicate is speech, and speech is not the same thing as the things that are perceptible (i.e., it is not light or sound, though light and sound may be used to convey written or spoken speech).

Furthermore, just as the perceptibles are not interchangeable, speech cannot be equated with that which exists, which is outside of us.

Therefore, speech can never exactly represent the perceptibles any more than the eye can hear or the hand smell.

Hence (just as the sense organs cannot give their information to any other sense organ), speech cannot give any information about anything perceptible—it gives only information about what is spoken.

Thus, if anything exists and is comprehensible, it is incommunicable.

Language is a Mighty Lord

Andrew J. Patrick

EPITAPHIOS

For what was absent in these men which should be present in men, and what things were present which should be absent?

Would that I could say what I wish and would that I might wish what I should say, evading the nemesis of the gods and avoiding the envy of men.

For these men possessed a virtue that was divine, a mortality that was human; oftentimes preferring the mildness of equity to the malignity of justice; oftentimes too, the righteousness of reason to the rigidity of law; considering the following to be the most godlike and most common code: aright at the fitting time either to speak or keep silence, either to act or to leave alone; cultivating (askeo) the duality especially that one ought to practice: judgment and strength; planning with the one and performing with the other; helper of those who unjustly suffered misfortune, and chastisers of those who were unjustly unfortunate; pitiless toward the profiteering, propitiating toward propriety, by the reasonableness of their judgment checking the unreasonableness of strength, violent toward the violators, moderate toward the moderate, gentle toward those who inspire no fear, terrible toward those who inspire terror.

As witnesses of these things they set up trophies over their enemies, statues of Zeus, votive gifts for themselves, not being ignorant of inborn courage nor lawful loves, nor strenuous strife nor honorable peace; reverent toward the gods in righteousness, filial toward their forbears in service, equitable toward their fellow citizens with equity, leal toward their friends with loyalty.

Therefore, when they die, yearning for them did not die, but deathless in bodies not immortal, lives for those no longer living.

Language is a Mighty Lord

Andrew J. Patrick

AN ENCOMIUM OF GORGIAS

"Famous men have the whole earth as their memorial," said Pericles in his *Funeral Oration*,[9] and he is testament to his own words. So long as human memory lasts, so long as Athens is more than a point on a map, Pericles will be remembered, as democracy's doomed champion, the statesman of the people. So also will Socrates be remembered, and Plato, and Aristotle, and Sophocles. They need no explanation among the educated; their very names are touchstones of civilization.

But under the penumbra of famous names on which history's light shines perpetual, there dwell a host of lesser names, which among the erudite provoke a nod of recognition, but hardly fame. However significant their contributions, however applauded their labors in their own time, to us they remain but a dim mark scratched deep in the palimpset of time.

To the eyes, clarity is best, to the tongue, refinement, to the memory, truth. Our sight and taste bring hourly new hints of awareness, new clues to the eternal. In this unfolding, the lucidity of yesterday is set aside for a new vision, the pleasures of yesterday for maturing detection. We spend our days chasing truth's fiery chariot, and every step takes us further away from the golden dawn.

Thus clarity and propriety alike drive us to embrace honesty, to examine our memory, to consider and re-consider what we have learned. And where particular visions have held dominance and sway over particular subjects, it behooves us to behold them again, that the truth of our memory be weighed and tested. In such a way, I intend to behold Gorgias the Sophist,[10] one of the lesser names of antiquity, and then to hold him up as worthy of praise, and unworthy of the accusations of baseness, as Plato and others since have leveled against him.[11]

---

[9] Thucydides, 2.43.

[10] W.C.K. Guthrie, *The Sophists* (Cambridge: Cambridge University Press, 1971), 273. Gorgias may have been a teacher of Pericles, or perhaps an associate.

[11] Catherine Osborne, *Presocratic Philosophy: A Very Short Introduction* (Oxford: Oxford University Press, 2004), 114. Osborne holds that while opinion of the Sophists in general have varied over the last 150 years, prior to the twentieth century they were "generally condemned for their subversive effects," excluding Nietsche, whose opinion on convention so closely mirrors Callicles' in Plato's *Gorgias*. With the advent

Plato's dialogues damned the Sophists as intellectual frauds, as traveling peddlers of philosophical snake-oil.[12] Yet of Gorgias of Leontini we must confess a sturdy intellectual pedigree. For tradition holds and scholarship cannot refute that he studied under the first generation of rhetoricians, Corax and Teisias, that he followed also the philosopher Empedocles, and that his brother Herodicas was a doctor. From the first, he learned his art, from the second, his science, and from the third, his sense of serving the public good.

Grafted from such stock, he possessed great skill, which he retained throughout his long life.[13] In many did he work desire for his skill, and his gifted tongue was the cause of bringing together many students and many drachma, by parents thinking great thoughts for great goals, some for maintaining greatness and wealth, some for gaining the glory of the ancient nobility, some of finding a fit use for a vigorous personality, and a few even of acquiring knowledge.[14] When old age ought to have wearied his bones, promising divine sleep, he instead captivated an Olympic audience with a speech urging the Greeks to seek peace that they may unite against Persia,[15] a dream that passed to his student Isocrates,[16] to Xenophon,[17] and thence to Alexander who fulfilled the prophecy.[18]

---

of the Cold War, however, the Sophists were re-branded as "champions of liberalism" while Plato became a quasi-Stalinist.

[12] Osborne titles her chapter on the Sophists "Spin Doctors of the 5th Century." Given Gorgias' tangential connection with the medical profession, one wonders whether he would have approved of the title.

[13] G.B. Kerferd, *The Sophistic Movement* (Cambridge: Cambridge University Press, 1981), 44. He sets the year of Gorgias' birth as around 485 B.C., while noting that he addressed the Athenian assembly in 427, to persuade the Athenians to make an alliance with Leontini against Syracuse, and was "much admired for his rhetorical skill," no small feat for a man nearing 60 in the ancient world. He died, according to tradition, some time in the early 4th Century.

[14] Kerferd, 15-23; Osborne 116. In his chapter about the Sophists as a social phenomenon, Kerferd points to the fact that they plied their trade to those that could afford them, and thus provided to the wealthy and powerful the precise means needed to govern a democratic state. Osborne concurs, pointing out that democratic leaders are quicker to engage in manipulation than monarchs or aristocrats.

[15] Will Durant, *The Life of Greece*, Vol. 2 of *The Story of Civilization* (New York: Simon and Schuster, 1939), 360. On the same page, Durant quotes Philostratus' *Lives of the Sophists*, which declared that "though Gorgias attained to the age of one hundred and eight, his body was not weakened by old age, but to the end of his life he was in sound condition, and his senses were those of a youth."

Having now introduced my subject, I shall set forth the causes through which it is likely that Gorgias has been condemned by scholars, and then I shall refute them. I consider these causes as being four in number: first, that Gorgias, even if a student of Empedocles, abused his instruction for profit, and was no philosopher; second, that Gorgias as a rhetorician taught lies, and taught men to embrace lies; third, that this influence upon the youth of Greece caused in part the decline of Greece, the degeneration of her liberty and culture; and fourth, that even his style of rhetoric is tedious to read, repellently stuffed with excess adornment, instead of elegant argument.

To the first charge, I admit that Gorgias has not the achievements that others of his day, called philosophers, do. He did not, for example, conclude from a chain of reasoning that the world was only water, as Thales did; nor air or fire, as Anaximenes and Heraclitus did. He did not tell men to ignore the evidence of their senses and agree with him that change and time do not exist, as Parmenides did, nor that motion is impossible, as Zeno did. He did not declare that the heavens in motion produced a sound that we could not hear because we hear nothing else, as the Pythagoreans did.[19] On this ground, Gorgias was no philosopher. Whether such philosophy would be of benefit to human understanding or Gorgias' reputation is another question.

If, however, one reads Empedocles and Gorgias closely, one will see the thoughts of the one in the other. With permission, and in respect, I cite Empedocles' teaching on Love and Strife, from his *Physics*:

> *I shall tell a twofold tale. Now they grew to be one alone from many, and now they grew apart again to be many from one. Double is the generation of mortal things, double their passing away;*

---

[16] Guthrie, 273.

[17] Durant, 488. Although Xenophon studied under Socrates, Isocrates the rhetorician seems to have had some influence on him as well.

[18] Arrian *The Campaigns of Alexander* 2.7. In his address to his army before the Battle of Issus, Arrian quotes Alexander as reminding them that Xenophon's Ten Thousand defeated the Persian army despite being smaller and lacking the cavalry and missile troops that the Macedonian army had.

[19] Aristotle, *On the Heavens* 290^{b}12-29.

the one is born and destroyed by the congregation of everything,
the other is nurtured and flies apart as they grow apart again.

And these never cease their continual change,
now coming together by Love all into one,
now again all being carried apart by the hatred of Strife.

Thus insofar as they have learned to become one from many,
and again become many as the one grows apart,
to that extent they come into being and have no lasting life;
but insofar as they never cease their continual interchange,
to that extent they exist forever, unmoving in a circle.

But come, hear my stories, for learning enlarges the mind.
As I said before, when I revealed the limits of my stores,
I shall tell a twofold tale. For now they grew to be one alone
from many, and now they few apart again to be many from one –
fire and water and earth and the boundless height of air,
and cursed Strife apart from them, balanced in every way,
and Love among them, equal in length and breadth.[20]

Admitting that the expression of verse differs from the expression of prose, as fire differs from air, we nevertheless must note the schemes of repetition that Gorgias' teacher uses. The eye clearly catches the opening isocolon, and the successive anaphora, schemes of repetition and of balance respectively. Such balance and repetition support, as water supported earth in Thales' theory, the philosopher's theme: that the world is a mixture of the same elements repeatedly coming together and repeatedly coming apart, eternally balanced. Though few call Empedocles a rhetorician,[21] his artistic sense of

---

[20] Jonathan Barnes, *Early Greek Philosophy* (London: Penguin Books, 2001), 120-121. Both Barnes and Osborne cite this fragment of Empedocles, and both write in the light of the recent discovery of the Strasbourg Papyrus that has added to scholarship of the philsopher. I cite Barnes' translation for reasons of both completeness and aesthetic pleasure; his versions *scans* better. The rhetorical schemes I point out are the same.

[21] Osborne, 10; Durant, 356. Here, citing "the stories," she refers to him as "a wonder-worker and magician, thinker and poet, medic and mystic," and mentions that he was "famous in antiquity for his fine poetry," but spares the professional title. On the other hand, Durant cites Diogenes Laertes to claim that Aristotle called Empedocles the inventor of rhetoric.

expression must surely have influenced his pupil. Shall we wonder then, that some historians have even claimed that Gorgias "studied philosophy *and rhetoric* with Empedocles?"[22]

But this comes as proof only for the proposition that Gorgias learned rhetoric from his master, not philosophy. For philosophers, the nature of thought commands not that ideas should obey expression, but that expression should serve ideas; we must then cease to speak further of the words until we learn the teaching of Empedocles.

Scholarship knows him as the first of the pluralists,[23] the first to break with the monists who flourished from Thales to Zeno,[24] and argue that the world was not made up of one substance but of four: Earth, Air, Water and Fire. Yet the *Physics* seems to hold these as secondary in nature to the ever-turning Love and Strife. And so Empedocles did: the four elements are eternal, but passive; Love and Strife likewise eternal, but eternally active.[25] It is they who drive the things of world; and all things, whatever their constitution, submit to being driven.

The true distinction, then, between Empedocles and the monists was not the number of physical elements he counted at the root of the world, but his belief that physical elements bow to spiritual ones. With permission, I continue to cite from the *Physics*, at the point of my earlier departure:

> *Her you must regard in thought: do not sit staring with your eyes.*
> *She is deemed to be innate also in mortal bodies,*
> *and by her they think friendly thoughts and perform deeds of*
> *peace, calling her Joy by name and Aphrodite,*
> *whom no on has seen as she whirls among them —*

---

[22] Durant, 360. The italics are mine.
[23] W.T. Jones, *The Classical Mind*, Vol. 1 of *A History of Western Philosophy* (New York: Harcourt, Brace, and Jovanovich, 1970), 28.
[24] Jones, 11. Even Anaximander, in some ways a precursor of Empedocles, was essentially a monist – earth, air, fire, and water were manifestations of the true, "boundless" substance.
[25] Jones, 26. Jones also suggests that Empedocles has borrowed Anaximander's dualisms – hot/cold, wet/dry – and applied them on a universal scale.

*no mortal man. But listen to the course of my argument, which
does not deceive,
these are all equal and of the same age,
but they hold different offices and each has its own character;
and they have power in turn as time revolves.*[26]

The gods, and one goddess in particular, here receive their due
from Empedocles. Love, or Aphrodite, comes forth from the mind of
the philosopher with several characteristics: one, that she is not
physical, two, that she is nevertheless found in all physical bodies, and
three, that she is the source of all deeds and thoughts considered
friendly, joyous, and peaceful. Strife, we may assume, is similar yet
opposed to her.

Let us then turn, having examined the master, to call upon the
work of the student, that both may be tested, the one for his
effectiveness, the other for his diligence. With hope that I am not
wearying your eyes, I cite from Gorgias' *Encomium of Helen*:

> *For either by will of Fate and decision of the Gods and vote of
> Necessity did she do what she did, or by force reduced or by words
> seduced or by love possessed. Now, if through the first, it is right
> for the responsible one to be held responsible; for god's
> predetermination cannot be hindered by human
> premeditation...God is a stronger force than man in might and in
> wit and in other ways. If one must place blame on Fate and on a
> god, one must free Helen from disgrace . . .*
>
> *If, therefore, the eye of Helen, pleased by the figure of Alexander,
> presented to her soul eager desire and contest of love, what wonder?
> If, being a god, love has the divine power of the gods, how could a
> lesser being reject and refuse it?*[27]

For the student as for the master, Love is a goddess, whose will is
doubly impossible for a mere mortal to counteract. Herein does
Empedocles' idea find expression in a practical circumstance, which is
the purpose and function of rhetoric. If Love drives all things, then
Helen could no more resist it than could a horse resist the harness.

---

[26] Barnes, 122.

[27] Gorgias, *Encomium of Helen* 6, 19.

Empedocles' philosophy expresses itself in other elements of the *Encomium of Helen*. Permit me to draw your eyes to the following:

> *But if it was speech which persuaded her and deceived her heart, not even to this is it difficult to make an answer and to banish blame as follows. Speech is a powerful lord, which by means of the finest and most invisible body effects the divinest works . . .*
>
> *Fearful shuddering and tearful pity and grievous longing come upon its hearers, and at the actions and physical sufferings of others in good fortunes and evil fortunes, through the agency of words, the soul is wont to experience a suffering of its own . . .*
>
> *Sacred incantations sung with words are bearers of pleasure and banishers of pain, for, merging with opinion in the soul, the power of the incantation is wont to beguile it and persuade it and alter it by witchcraft . . .* [28]

Speech, to Gorgias, is an agent of the gods, "a powerful lord" summoning pain or pleasure, according to whether Eris[29] or Aprhodite command him. As Empedocles would put it, words mix with the elements innate to the human soul and move the human will according to the divine will. The human soul thus is "constrained" by speech.[30] The master, were he called upon to defend Helen, could scarcely have put it better.

But it may still be asked if using Empedocles' philosophy in epideictic speech makes Gorgias a philosopher. I answer in the words of Gorgias' accuser, Plato, from his dialogue called *Gorgias*:

> *SOCRATES: Well now, a man who has learned building is a builder, is he not?*
> *GORGIAS: Yes.*
> *SOCRATES: And he who has learned music, a musician?*

---

[28] Gorgias, *Encomium of Helen* 8,9,10.

[29] Kerferd, 34. Plato called the "Socratic method" of question-and-answer *Dialectic*, whereas that of the sophists he named *Eristic*, for the Goddess of Discord. Plato makes the distinction that he is seeking shared understanding by *dialogue*, whereas the sophists are seeking victory in verbal combat. Eris' place in Greek mythology, in the Iliad and elsewhere, makes her a fit counterpart for Aphrodite.

[30] Gorgias, 12.

GORGIAS: Yes.
SOCRATES: Then he who has learned music is a medical
man, and so on with the rest on the same principle; anyone who
has learned a certain art has the qualification acquired by his
particular knowledge?
GORGIAS: Certainly.[31]

Plato's principle is clear: he who learns a skill merits the title to which that skill is attached. So one who learns philosophy is a philosopher. We might add a second criterion: that the student puts the subject into practice, and demonstrates his knowledge. If so, happy for Gorgias! For he has studied the pluralist philosophy of Empedocles, applied it in practical circumstances, and expanded the notion to include phenomena the master did not – specifically, speech as a Divine Agent.[32] For what reason, then, can anyone withhold from Gorgias the title of Philosopher?[33]

Having disposed of the first charge, that Gorgias perverted Empedocles' teachings and was no philosopher, I proceed to the second: that Gorgias taught lies and lying. If this were so, it were indeed a grievous fault; but a clear-eyed investigation will be sufficient to prove that it is not so.

In the process, I will make what some may consider a narrow distinction: the stipulative difference between a lie, and something false. By a lie, we mean an attempt to make a person believe something that the persuader knows not to be true, so the person changes his will to the persuader's advantage. Certainly, no defense can be mustered for

---

[31] Plato, *Gorgias* p. 95

[32] Barnes, 140; 154. Empedocles has little to say on the subject of speech, even in his fragments pertaining to perception and thought. In fact, his description of gods holds their minds to be "holy and unutterable," which may put some distance between Gorgias and his teacher on the significance of speech. He would not be the first student to thus alter what he has learned by his own perception.

[33] Kerferd, 35-36 argues that the real reason has to do with the fact that the Sophists left few surviving scholarly works, being as they were chiefly involved with instruction. In this sense the difference between the Sophists and the Platonic and Aristotelian "schools" is analogous to the difference between a primary/secondary school instructor, called a "teacher," and a college/university instructor, or "professor."

this practice; lies are the distorters of human minds and the corruptors of their hearts.

Plato makes this charge not only against Gorgias, but against the entire practice of rhetoric: he likens rhetoric to cookery, which persuades by pleasure the eating of unhealthy things.[34] Far from instructing with truth on matters of law or policy, rhetoric simply aims to convince their wills of what the orator desires. They come away not enlightened, but enslaved.

The difficulty in refuting this characterization of rhetoric is that Gorgias himself in some way has admitted to it. Witness the following:

> *All who have and do persuade people of things do so by molding a false argument. For if all men on all subjects had both memory of things past and awareness of things present and foreknowledge of the future, speech would not be similarly similar . . . . So that on most subjects most men take opinion as the counselor to their soul, but since opinion is slippery and insecure it casts those employing it into slippery and insecure successes.*[35]

One wonders why Plato strains so mightily against Gorgias to establish what Gorgias so magnanimously gives him. But the greater of wonders is why a rhetorician, in the midst of a rhetorical address, should so deliberately break the spell he weaves, and cast doubt not just on his present argument, but on his entire life's work!

One possible answer is that Gorgias made the argument as a rhetorical device, to expand his *ethos* by sharing with his audience what he was doing. In this manner, Gorgias compliments his audience on *not* being fooled, that they, like he, were aware of the power of words, and hence, he could not use their power on *them*. But this answer fails to encompass his admission: not only rhetorical speech, but *all* speech, is "a mighty Lord," and all persuasion based on falsehood. As Gorgias at this moment attempts to persuade of Helen's innocence, he at this moment, by his own admission, molds a false argument.

---

[34] Plato, *Gorgias* 98
[35] Gorgias *Encomium of Helen* 11

We have earlier granted Gorgias the name of a philosopher; let us likewise grant that in making this admission, he, like Plato, is thinking as one. Let us therefore assume his aware and intent of this admission as the salient point of his speech. We incline to accept this, given that the other arguments – That Helen cannot be blamed if Fate, physical force, or irrational love carried her away to Troy – excite far less controversy.

If his description of speech as a dangerous and powerful weapon, working upon the mind like a drug, makes up his main point, we may conclude that this point, far from being a rhetorical tactic or feather in the cap of his cleverness, was a deeply held belief. For men fear to excite controversy, as unpredictable in effect as war, save for the sake of some greater good. Hence, for Gorgias the Rhetorician to claim that rhetoric, and indeed all speech, lack truth, he must have been fully convinced of it.

Deep are the minds of ancient philosophers, and as other deep things, darkly lit and difficult to explore. Of the numerous writings attributed to Gorgias,[36] only a few survive: the *Helen*, the *Apology of Palamedes*, and his *On Nature, or What is Not*. If we are to detect a held doctrine on speech in the mind of Gorgias, we do so on these promontories.

Fortunately, a common thread does come to light. To illustrate it, I will cite, ever briefly, first from the *Apology of Palamedes*, then from *On Nature*. The first of these, a defense of the captain in the *Iliad* accused of treason by Odysseus, is a prose translation and an example of an argument from probability,[37] which, as Aristotle argued, is the essence of rhetoric.[38] Here I present my concise selections:

---

[36] John Dillon and Tania Gergel, *The Greek Sophists* (London: Penguin Books Ltd., 2003), 44; Kerferd, 44; Guthrie, 270. The list includes his *Funeral Oration*, of which a fragment remains, his *Olympian Oration*, the *Pythian Oration*, and the *Encomium of Elis*, in addition to the surviving works. Kerferd believes it probable that he wrote a treatise on rhetoric called *Art* or *On the Right Moment in Time*, as well as an *onomastikon*, or collection of proper names and terms. On the other hand, Guthrie denies that Gorgias had any interest in the creation of any *orthopedia*, in contrast to Protagoras and Prodicus.

[37] Dillon and Gergel, 84.

[38] Aristotle *Rhetoric* 1.1.1356^b.32

Are you attacking me on the basis of sure knowledge or of conjecture?[39]

It is open, surely, for all men to have opinions on any subject you please, and as to this you are no wiser than anyone else; but it is not right to repose trust in those who express opinions, but rather in those that have knowledge, nor to hold opinion to be more trustworthy than truth, but on the contrary, truth more trustworthy than opinion.[40]

It is not proper to resort to persuasion by means of the intercession of friends or entreaties or appeals to pity, but it is right for me to escape this charge by relying on the most perspicuous justice, explaining the truth, not seeking to deceive you. And you in your turn should not give more credence to words in preference to deeds . . . nor believe that slander is more reliable than your experience of me.[41]

The theme is unmistakable: Gorgias delineates between what can be said, and what is true, and defines conjecture and emotive persuasion as inferior to reasoned argument. Yet all Greeks knew that Palamedes failed in his attempt to exonerate himself and was executed by the army; despite his reason, Odysseus' pernicious slander held sway. Here again, and with the same great tale, Gorgias warns us of the power of speech. Indeed, we may be pardoned for wondering whether Gorgias saw anything of value in the art to which he devoted his life and from which earned his livelihood. But he has given us just such an indication, at the close of the *Apology*:

If then, through words the truth of deeds could become transparent and manifest to one's hearers, judgement would be easy on the basis of what has been said. Since, however, this is not the case, put a guard on my body . . .[42]

We may thus draw the common thread: on the one hand there is truth and knowledge, on the other, *doxa*, or opinion, and *logos*, or

---

[39] Gorgias *Apology of Palamedes* 22
[40] Ibid., 24
[41] Ibid, 33, 34
[42] Gorgias *Apology of Palamedes* 35

speech. Both *logos* and *doxa* are essentially deceptive, but just as Palamedes must defend himself by speech, truth must be appealed to by *logos*.[43] And as both the truth and falsehood can be spoken aloud, we must distinguish between good and evil speech. One comes away from the *Apology* with the hopeful conclusion that had Palamedes been there, he could have persuaded Helen to remain with her true lord.

The idea that speech necessarily deceives, first seen in the *Encomium*, and again in the *Apology*, is made explicit in *On Nature*. The first part of this treatise aims, like the bright point of a spear, directly at the throat of the Eleatic philosophy of being: If something has being, it is either single or multiple. If single, it is really multiple, as any quantity is divisible, any coninuum is severable, and any magnitude has itself three quantities of length, width and depth. Therefore, since all these things are part of having being, nothing that is single, lacking these things, has being. If, on the other hand, it is multiple, then it has no being either, since anything multiple is by definition composed of things that are single. Therefore, nothing that exists has being.[44]

Whatever the intent of this troubling argument,[45] it is the final part of *On Nature* that speaks to our subject:

> *Language is that by means of which we communicate, but language is not the objects and things out there. So we don't communicate the things out there to our neighbors. We communicate language, which is something other than the objects. And so just as what is seen could not come to be something heard and vice versa, so also since the things themselves lie outside us,*

---

[43] Kerferd, 81-82

[44] Gorgias, *On Nature* 73.

[45] Kerferd, 93-97; Osborne, 128-130. Scholarly opinion has varied about *On Nature* over the centuries. The longest-held view, according to Kerferd, is that it was nothing more than a joke or parody of the Eleatics. Then came the opinion that Gorgias seriously intended to argue the anti-Eleatic paradox that being did not exist. Most recently, the argument has become that, as Parmenides was less interested in distinguishing between existence and non-existence than between modes of definition, Gorgias was counter-arguing that the positive statements Parmenides favored contained similar contradictions to the negative statements he denounced. For her part, Osborne maintains that Gorgias was writing a philosophical satire displaying important truths about language.

the could not come to be our language; but since they are not language, they cannot be communicated to one another.[46]

Here again, we find the rhetorician casting wide the chasm between language and reality, between truth and words. We find ourselves constrained to conclude then, that when Gorgias argued that speech was so powerful a force as to exonerate Helen from blame for the Trojan War, and to convict Palamedes unjustly during the same war, he was using these events to make a point about a deeply held conviction, and thus we face the impossibility of his lying.

Rather, we here make our distinction, with Gorgias' help, between a lie and something false. The former is an attempt to deceive, the latter is but an expression erroneous or incomplete. If we accept Gorgias' notion that language incompletely expresses the fullness of any thing it attempts to describe, if we agree with him that language is limited; we agree that, to the extent any speech claims to express the whole truth, it is deceptive, because no speech can. Gorgias, in all of his works that survive, takes pains to point out this limitation, or falsehood, of language. And to point out a falsehood is but to speak a truth.

So much for the charge that Gorgias taught lies. I turn now to the third charge, that Gorgias, being a Sophist, was a corruptor of Greek culture at the moment of its glory, a Serpent in the Garden. This charge, if true, would seem the worst, for it would mean that whatever Gorgias intended, he caused harm; whatever the fine flourish of his phrases, or plausibility of his pronouncements, if the result of their being heeded was the decay of civilization, he deserves scorn from all thinking humans.

Yet if we trust our reasoning thus far, the charge strains credulity. To argue that a man, worthy of the title of philosopher, who taught a reasonable point about language caused, even in part, the downfall of a culture is enough to make one doubt the value of philosophy or reason. The only way we could put the argument plausibly would be to claim that rhetoric of the kind that Gorgias taught brought about the decline of philosophy and reason, causing both to sink into pedantism and fallacy.

---

[46] Gorgias, *On Nature* 84-85

If so, where is the evidence for such a claim? Did schools of philosophy disappear from Athens after Gorgias' time? Did important philosophers cease their investigation into the nature of the universe and of humanity, cut down by the grim *eristic* of the *Encomium of Helen*?

To ask the question is to answer it, for we know that exactly the opposite happened. In Athens, Gorgias' pupil Isocrates founded perhaps the first great school of liberal arts,[47] and some few years later, Plato's Academy began teaching mathematics and metaphysics free of charge.[48] And during the conquests of Alexander,[49] Aristotle built the Lyceum, offering rhetoric, poetry, ethics and politics while a zoo and a natural history museum sprang up behind him.[50] Shall we not speak truth and say that in the years following Gorgias' death, Greek philosophy flourished?

It would be as unreasonable to assign too much credit to Gorgias for these fine developments as it would be to assign blame to him for the true cultural decline of Greece that began in the Hellenistic epoch. For, leaving aside the contributions of the school of Isocrates, Plato and Aristotle hardly owe to Gorgias anything for their achievements.

Or do they?

We have not the time, after such discussion as has already been engaged in, to delve deeply into a complete history of Hellenic Philosophy. Yet it will not take long to determine that in this history patterns form that, like the arrangement of candles in a cathedral, illuminate the significant features, even for those whose visit is brief.

Thus, we will not be long in perceiving that the great and powerful philosophers of Greece, thaumaturges of thought, were in constant conflict with one another. What would have become of the famed philosophy of the Greeks, had Anaximander not disputed with Thales the foundation of the world? Or if Empedocles had not contradicted Parmenides and Zeno? Or even if Aristotle had not "refuted Plato at every turn because he borrowed from him on every page?"[51]

---

[47] Durant, 485-486.
[48] Ibid., 511.
[49] Ibid., 525. And perhaps, with the conqueror's financial assistance.
[50] Ibid.

Indeed, if there exists a force of logic by which we shall not ask "Without the questions of the Sophists, could Plato have ever constructed his great answers,"[52] let it now come forward, and I will bow to it. Lacking this, I think it meet and fitting to state plainly that, as Thales provoked Anaximander, as Parmenides provoked Empedocles, so Gorgias provoked Socrates,[53] and we are all the beneficiaries.[54]

Let me then consider the third charge well refuted, and take up the fourth. I have considered it closely, for it may be the most difficult yet to prove with satisfaction. To call a man a philosopher, you can point to his studies; to call him honest, you can point to his conviction; to call him beneficial, you can point to those who harvested what he sowed. But to call him a fine writer is to leave such easy factual foundations behind.

The difficulty arises when I realize my task as making an argument from my own opinion, countering it against the opinion of those who have passed judgment already. For what do men cling to with greater violence, than their opinions? And justly so, for what is an opinion but the fruit of your own mind's consideration? To surrender it to another without struggle would be as shameful as to offer up the city walls upon the sight of the first rider. How grim, then, for Gorgias, and how foolish for myself if, after these labors I shall find myself forced to admit Gorgias a poor stylist; after burnishing the image of his philosophy, I cannot defend the music of his language!

---

[51] Ibid, 524.

[52] Anthony Gottlieb, *The Dream of Reason* (New York: W.W. Norton & Company, 2000), 126; Dillon & Gergel, xix; Guthrie, 21; Osborne, 131. All of these make more or less the same argument, that the Sophists "ask the questions" about all assumptions regarding the nature of human reason and human souls, and the Socratics "answered them" by developing new understandings of these same topics.

[53] Guthrie, 272. Guthrie offers an explanation for why Plato's dialogue is named for Gorgias by suggesting that "Whereas rhetoric was in the curriculum of every Sophist, Gorgias must have put it more prominently in his shop window than any of the others." Considering the respectful tone that Socrates adopts toward Gorgias in the dialogue, in contrast to the gentle mocking that others, such as Polus gets, Plato seems to have intended that the master was responsible for the younger generation.

[54] To say nothing of the rather obvious notion that that the rhetorical skill of the Sophists prompted Aristotle, ever in conflict with Plato, to defend and formalize rhetoric as an art form.

Yet some commonality remains in our words, that I may hope to persuade that praise of Gorgias' style of oratory, rather than blame, is just. And I trust, when my order of battle will appear, that the strength of my opinion will become clear.

Gorgias commences his *Encomium of Helen* with a running isocolon, broad in scope and ethical in subject, on what is best for cities, bodies, souls, actions, and speeches. From long scheme to short, he reverses the order of these things into a polysyndeton: "Man and woman and speech and deed and city and object. . . . "[55] before tying them to the unremarkable antithesis that they should be blamed or praised as worthy. Thus, Gorgias starts his speech in slow solemnity, not merely calling upon broad principles, as Homer calling upon the muses, but demanding the audience pay close attention to what they doubtless consider tediously obvious: that things "should be honored with praise if unworthy, for it is an equal error and mistake to blame the praisable and to praise the blamable."[56]

Whence this lens-grinding? Gorgias' detractors would scoff at this as but the sound of air leaving a wineskin, the sound and fury that signifies nothing. But we, who have considered the philosophy behind Gorgias' rhetoric, know better. By opening with obvious maxims, he calls his audience to duty, reminds them of what is right, and that such things can be easily forgotten, especially under the force of skillful speech, which, as he also reminds us in the opening isocolon, ought to have truth. As we have seen before, his rhetoric serves his philosophy of language.

In what follows, Gorgias blends sound and meaning skillfully, alternating assonance and polyptoton:

> . . . *a woman about whom the testimony of inspired poets has become univocal and unanimous . . . I wish to free the accursed of blame and, having reproved her detractors as prevaricators and proved the truth, to free her from ignorance.*[57]

---

[55] Gorgias, *Encomium of Helen* 1.
[56] Ibid.
[57] Gorgias, *Encomium of Helen* 2.

Whatever this may miss in imaginative reason, it lacks not liveliness, nor linguistic pleasure. It does not roll, but dances, off the tongue, almost so pleased with itself as to suggest a sly wink, as only the author of a treatise called *What is Not* could.

Were I to go on through the nineteen remaining paragraphs of the *Encomium*, I would quickly exhaust my remaining claim of brevity. It would follow much the same: polyptoton, assonance, and alliteration, spiced with parallelism and polysyndeton, leavened with occasional antithesis or chiasmus, mix freely in the same sentence, even within the same clause.[58]

Oddly, a speech so brimming with schemes is all but bereft of tropes. Hardly a meaning is substituted for another, save with careful attention. I can find but three metaphors in the whole of the *Encomium*:

> *Speech is a powerful lord. . .*

> *. . . the words of astronomers who, substituting opinion for opinion, taking away one but creating another, make what is incredible and unclear seem true to the eyes of opinion . . .*

> *The effect of speech upon the condition of the soul is comparable to the power of drugs over the nature of bodies.*[59]

Gorgias summons all of these to bolster and explain his central argument about the power and danger of language. As a trope deviates from a word's ordinary signification, while a scheme, its ordinary arrangement, what can we conclude from Gorgias' use of both in a speech focused on language?

First, we must conclude that Gorgias was aware of what he was doing. Figures of speech were used before they were classified, not classified and then used.[60] If Gorgias altered the pattern of his words

---

[58] In my count of schemes, polyptoton and alliterations tie at seven uses each, followed by six of isocolon, four each of polysyndeton, assonance, and parallelism, and two each of antithesis and rhyme.
[59] Gorgias, *Encomium of Helen* 8, 13, 14.
[60] Edward P.J. Corbett and Robert J. Connors, *Classical Rhetoric for the Modern Student* (Oxford: Oxford University Press, 1999), 378-379.

far more than their signification, we may feel safe in saying that such was his intent.[61] Why, then, would he have intended thus?

The *Encomium* still entertains, millennia after its context, chiefly because it cheekily demonstrates what it condemns; it decries the use of language to distort the senses, yet in passionate and overflowing style, heavy with schemes. For it is a scheme that, by changing the arrangement of phrases, gives the words a symphonic force beyond their individual meanings.

The essence of the Gorgiastic style is musicality, a rhythmic performance in which the pleasure given to the audience appeals to their *pathos* and his *ethos* simultaneously, the one inclining their emotions to enjoy without analysis, the other suggesting that one who has taken the time to so polish his words knows the matter well enough to make an art of it. That is, eloquence demonstrates good sense in the rhetorician *qua* rhetorician, and goodwill towards his audience in arranging something for their pleasure.[62]

This very musicality may be the cause of some of the antipathy with which the Gorgiastic style meets. For this, Gorgias has no one but himself to blame: we have largely absorbed his argument about the seductive danger of speech. When someone crafts a clearly and obviously well-polished address, we oft incline more to distrust the speaker's motive, rather than to trust his knowledge.

But this depends upon how *obvious* the crafting is; a well-crafted speech that speaks to the audience on the level they operate on does well. Gorgias' works may well strike the modern reader as too eloquent, too elevated; if the ancient prejudice held that craft marked quality, the modern has decided that nothing which shines too brightly has substance.

But to argue from this that the Asian style is forever buried while the Attic forever supreme is difficult. For one thing, it ignores the

---

[61] Obviously, Gorgias' writings and speeches reflected the civilization in which he lived. An analysis of the use of schemes and tropes by all the 4th Century Sophists might reveal a prediliction for schemes. However, Gorgias was a teacher and not merely a user of rhetoric, and everything we've established about him leads us to believe that he thought about it quite seriously.

[62] Aristotle, *Rhetoric* II.1.1378a.

history of the styles: When the "Asian" style becomes the "Ciceronian," and the "Attic" the "Senecan," does this not suggest a cyclical trend in relative popularity? Not long ago for us, but centuries beyond the time of the Sophists, Edmund Burke wrote prose as florid and ornate as any by Gorgias, as crammed with polyptoton, parallelism, and antithesis, and as cagily aware of the seductive power of unreflective speech:

> *When the old feudal and chivalrous spirit of Fealty, which, by freeing kings from fear, freed kings and subjects from the precautions of tyranny, shall be extinct from the minds of men, plots and assassinations will be anticipated by preventive murder and preventive confiscation, and that long roll of grim and bloody maxims, which form the political code of all power, not standing on its own honour, and the honor of those who are to obey it. Kings will be tyrants from policy when subjects are rebels from principle.*[63]

That Thomas Paine mocked Burke's style as hysterical and "a dramatic performance,"[64] does not take away a jot of its effectiveness,[65] nor does it establish that the "Burkean style"[66] will forever be out of style. In fiction, for example, a musical approach to language often wins laurels. Witness, if you will, the following selection from the critically-praised novel *Blood Meridian* by Cormac McCarthy, author of *No Country for Old Men* and *The Road*:

> *They rode up through cholla and nopal, a dwarf forest of spined things, though a gap in the mountains and down among blooming Artemisia and aloe. They crossed a broad plain of desert frass dotted with palmilla. On the slopes were gray stone walls that*

---

[63] Edmund Burke, *Reflections on the Revolution in France* (Mineola: Dover Publications, 2006), 77. Note the "grim and bloody maxims," an almost Gorgiastic expression connecting speech with dangerous power.

[64] Thomas Paine, *The Rights of Man* (New York: ClassicBooksAmerica, 2009), 27.

[65] Ibid. Paine, in fact, underhandedly admits as much when he writes that:"It suits his purposes to exhibit the consequences without their causes. It is one of the arts of drama to do so."

[66] To give the Asian / Ciceronian a title of more recent coinage. Christening the Attic / Senecan style as "Painian," would probably not work as well, he is not quite periodic enough. We might have to do with "Hemingwayan," in which case the Asian style might better be called "Faulknerian."

*followed the ridgelines down to where they lay broached and
tumbled upon the plain. They did not noon, nor did they siesta
and the cotton eye of the moon squatted at broad day in the throat
of the mountains to the east and they were still riding when it
overtook them at its midnight meridian, sketching on the plain
below a blue cameo of such dread pilgrims clanking north.*[67]

To be sure, differences abound between McCarthy's style and
Gorgias', in the use of schemes and of commas, but if McCarthy is not
quite Gorgiastic, neither is he Attic. His books have been praised for
precisely this rhythmic artistry.[68] Why, then, should we concede the
tyranny of the transitory, and consider the unfashionable blameworthy?
Aristotle himself says that all variations of style can be "used in season
or out of season."[69]

For his part, Gorgias was not without praise from the critics of his
day, by which we mean chiefly Aristotle. We might expect Aristotle to
condemn Gorgias in the *Rhetoric*, and he does, but commends him
more. Aristotle refers to Gorgias no less than nine times in the *Rhetoric*.[70]
Of them, fully five are positive, recommending Gorgias' various
techniques to his students, most notably his use of irony and humor.[71]
Of the remaining, two criticize him on stylistic grounds, for use of
extravagant compound words[72] or metaphors,[73] while another chides
him for making *too casual* a beginning to his *Encomium of Elis*.[74] The first

---

[67] Cormac McCarthy, *Blood Meridian, or The Evening Redness in the West* (New York:
Vintage International, 1992), 88.
[68] McCarthy has been called "the literary child of Faulkner" by *New Republic* magazine,
and his style "lyrical" by the *Times Literary Supplement*. Nothing is new under the sun.
[69] Aristotle *Rhetoric* III.7.1408ª.35
[70] He refers to Plato the same number of times. By contrast, the rhetorician
Thrasymachus is mentioned only four times, Antiphon three times, Corax, Prodicus,
and Hippias once each, and Teisias not at all.
[71] Aristotle *Rhetoric* III.3.1406ᵇ, III.7.1408ᵇ, III.18.1419ᵇ. Gorgias apparently had
enough self-composure to crack a sharp jest even when a swallow dropped its
leavings on him during a speech. The details of the story suggest that Aristotle had
either personally witnessed or it had become legendary in Athens. Given Gorgias'
wide travels, neither can be ruled out.
[72] Ibid III.2.1405ᵇ.
[73] Ibid III.2.1406ᵇ. And here, Aristotle takes exception on the grounds that the
metaphor is too poetical to work in a rhetorical situation, not that it is bad in itself.
[74] Ibid III.14.1416ª.

reference to Gorgias, an explanation of why oratical language "at first took on a poetical colour, e.g. that of Gorgias,"[75] does not bear the marks of a lashing. Aristotle seems to have understood that all things have their time.

And indeed, so did Gorgias. As a final argument, I feel compelled to point out that the great orator is credited with being the first to write about *kairos*, the right or proper moment, in regards to rhetoric. This is according to Dionysius of Halicarnassus, who further adds that *kairos* cannot be known objectively, but is a matter of *doxa*, of opinion.[76] If this is true, then the approving references of Gorgias in the *Rhetoric* are no accident, but a sign of how seriously he was taken as a rhetorician and orator, and how greatly his understanding of rhetoric figured into Aristotle's. Perhaps, rather than lazily lumping Gorgias among the teeming masses of "Pre-Socratics," we should assign him his true significance, as Pre-Aristotelian.

Permit me to pause now, ever briefly, to take stock of what I have offered. I have shown that Gorgias was a true student of Empedocles, who applied his teacher's learning. I have shown that Gorgias' work was centered on a significant truth on the nature of language and reality, which stimulated others to answer him with great vigor, to the everlasting fame of the Greeks. I have followed Aristotle in praising his eloquence where and when he was eloquent. I have argued the clarity of his eye, the refinement of his tongue, and his place among the deserving in human memory.

---

[75] Ibid III.1.1404ª.
[76] Kerferd, 82.

Language is a Mighty Lord

BIBLIOGRAPHY

1. Barnes, Johnathan. *Early Greek Philsophy*. London: Penguin Books, 2001.
2. Dillon, John, and Gergel, Tania. *The Greek Sophists*. London: Penguin Books, 2003.
3. Durant, Will. *The Life of Greece*, Vol. 2 of *The Story of Civilization*. New York: Simon & Schuster, 1939.
4. Gottlieb, Anthony. *The Dream of Reason: A History of Philosophy From The Greeks to the Renaissance*. New York: W.W. Nortony & Company, 2000.
5. Guthrie, W.C.K. *The Sophists*. Cambridge: Cambridge University Press, 1971.
6. Jones, W.T. *The Classical Mind*, Vol. 1 of *A History of Western Philosophy*. New York: Harcourt, Brace, & Jovanovich, 1970.
7. Kerferd, G.B. *The Sophistic Movement*. Cambridge: Cambridge University Press, 1981.
8. Osborne, Catherine. *Presocratic Philosophy: A Very Short Introduction*. Oxford: Oxford University Press, 2004.

ABOUT THE EDITOR

Andrew J. Patrick holds a Bachelor's Degree in International Relations from St. Joseph's University and a Master's Degree in Professional Writing from Towson University.. He resides in Maryland with his wife and daughter.

To find him online, go to andrewjpatrick.com, or @ajpwriter on Twitter.

www.ingramcontent.com/pod-product-compliance
Lightning Source LLC
Chambersburg PA
CBHW060717030426
42337CB00017B/2910